Discard

ASTRONOMY

Contents

A GOLDEN **EXPLORING EARTH** BOOK

ASTRONOMY
Our Sun and Its Neighbors

The wonders of the solar system and our earth's place
in it…the how and why of time and seasons…the vastness
of space and the galaxies, planets, moons, comets,
asteroids, and meteors that are found in it.

By Jene Lyon
Editorial Consultant: Diane M. Pyper, Ph. D.
University of Wisconsin — Parkside
Illustrated by George Solonewitsch and others
Cover by Rod Ruth

gb. GOLDEN PRESS

Western Publishing Company, Inc.   Racine, Wisconsin

Revised edition. Previously published as
OUR SUN AND THE WORLDS AROUND IT.

GOLDEN PRESS®, GOLDEN, and A GOLDEN EXPLORING EARTH BOOK are trademarks of
Western Publishing Company, Inc.

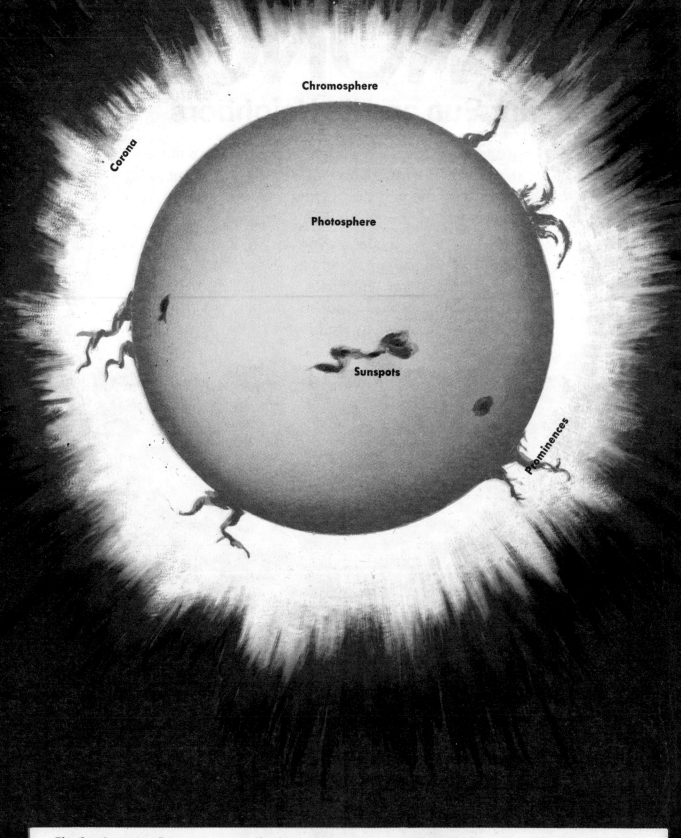

The Sun in space. From outer space, the Sun would appear as a giant ball of fire in an almost black sky. By using special equipment, scientists are able to see the main parts of the Sun named in this picture. The Sun's diameter—the distance from one side to the other, through the center—is 865,000 miles. Since the Earth is only 7,927 miles in diameter, it would take 109 Earths in a row to stretch across the Sun's face.

OUR SUN: THE NEAREST STAR

EVERY DAY the Sun crosses our sky. Even when it is hidden by clouds, we know it is there. At night we know it is still in the sky. Our side of the Earth has turned away from it.

The Sun was in the sky long before there were any people on the Earth, before dinosaurs roamed the prehistoric swamps, before there was any life at all on our planet. And it is because of the Sun that plants and animals and people can live on the Earth.

The Sun is a star, like those you see in the sky on a dark night. All stars are giant balls of very hot, churning gases. Some stars are blue, some red, some white. Our star—our Sun—is yellow.

Our Sun looks much larger than other stars because it is much nearer to us. The stars of the night sky are so far away that light from them takes years to reach us. Light from the Sun reaches us in about 8 minutes.

The Sun is about 93 million miles away—3,700 times the distance around the Earth at the equator. The Sun, though much nearer than other stars, is very far away indeed.

To us the Sun looks bright, but not large. Actually our Earth is just a speck compared to the Sun. If hollow, the Sun could hold a million Earths.

The Sun is made up mostly of the gases hydrogen and helium. It also contains many other materials known on Earth, such as iron, calcium, and sodium.

These substances are all so hot that they are in the form of glowing gases.

The bright surface of the Sun is called the photosphere. Its temperature is about 11,000 degrees—over 8,000 degrees hotter than the temperature needed to melt iron. The layer of glowing gases around the photosphere, known as the chromosphere, is thousands of miles deep. From it tongues of flame, sometimes a million miles long, leap out into space. Be thankful that Earth is far enough away!

Surrounding the chromosphere is the corona, a brilliant halo of light. Because of the photosphere's brightness, the corona can not be seen. Only by using special equipment or when a total eclipse hides the photosphere, does the corona become visible.

Heat from the Sun. How much heat do Sun rays have? Use a magnifying glass to "funnel" some Sun rays to a point. They will quickly burn paper or wood.

What we owe the Sun. The Sun gives us light, heat, and energy. It causes weather. Oil and coal contain energy received from the Sun by plants and animals long ago. Upon the Sun depend the lives of plants, animals, and people.

THE SUN'S ENERGY

We say the Sun is on fire, but this is not ordinary fire. Most of the Sun is made up of hydrogen gas atoms, which the heat—millions of degrees at the Sun's core—drives into wild commotion. Atoms crashing into each other may break up. Some parts join to form new atoms of the gas called helium. Other parts shoot off into space like sprays of little bullets. They are the so-called radiant energy that comes to us as sunlight.

The change of hydrogen into helium is just what happens when a hydrogen bomb explodes. But the bomb explosion is nothing compared to what happens in the Sun. Here, four million tons of hydrogen are turned into energy every second.

No wonder the Sun is so hot! But will it soon burn up? Astronomers say no. The Sun has been burning for billions of years and has enough hydrogen fuel for billions of years more.

Without this solar energy, our planet would be as cold as Pluto, the planet farthest from the Sun. That's something like 460 degrees below zero—much too cold for animals or plants to live. The inside of Earth is very hot, but the heat that gets to the crust is slight compared to what we get from the Sun.

Earth is so tiny in the immensity of space that only a small part of the Sun's radiant energy reaches us. Much of it is blocked by the atmosphere.

When sunlight hits the atmosphere, it

divides up into light rays of different colors. A blue sky is due to the scattering of blue rays through the atmosphere. Rainbows and colorful sunsets also are due to the scattering of sunlight.

On the Sun's photosphere darkish patches called sunspots sometimes appear. They shoot off particles of electrical energy which may interfere with radio and television communication on Earth and change our weather, too.

Some of the energy from the Sun is in the form of deadly rays like those from a hydrogen bomb. Luckily, most of these rays are stopped by our atmosphere.

Some Sun rays do get through to Earth's surface, and we can be glad they do. Plants use sunlight, soil, water, and air to manufacture the substances that man and animals eat. Without sunlight, plants could not grow. Without plants, no animal or human life could exist.

We can thank the Sun for our rains. Sun-heated air carries moisture from seas, lakes, and rivers up into the sky.

Winds carry it over land, and finally it forms clouds and falls as rain.

Some water runs underground, and we get it by means of wells. Some runs into the rivers, which carry it toward the sea again. On the way it may be dammed up and used by us for water power.

We get Sun energy also from coal and oil. Coal comes from masses of fallen plants that built up in prehistoric swamps. Oil comes from the remains of billions upon billions of tiny prehistoric water plants.

In the future mankind may get much power from atomic energy. This energy is obtained from minerals found in the Earth. But for a long time to come we shall surely depend on the Sun for most of our energy needs.

Radio, television, and weather on Earth are affected by sunspots. Some sunspots are 50,000 miles wide.

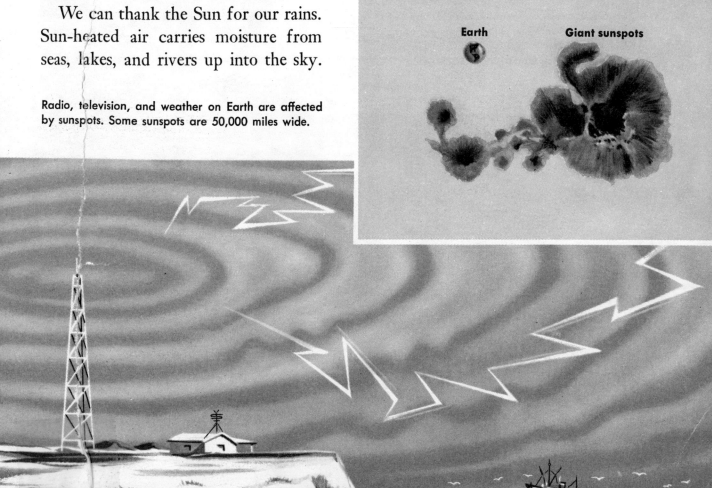

Earth

Giant sunspots

ECLIPSES OF THE SUN

ONE OF the most awe-inspiring sights in the world is an eclipse of the Sun. An eclipse occurs when the Moon passes directly between Earth and Sun. For the few minutes that the Sun is hidden from us, the Earth is dark and chill, and it may seem like the end of the world.

Some people in ancient times feared that an eclipse really did mean the end of the world. In China they believed that a dragon was eating up the Sun. Few people knew enough about Earth, Sun, and Moon to realize that what was happening was entirely harmless — and a sight to be enjoyed for its majesty.

The safest way to view an eclipse is by making a pinhole in a thin piece of cardboard. This hole acts as a lens when held up to the sun, and will form an image that can be seen on a white surface.

During an eclipse, first a shallow notch slowly appears at the edge of the Sun. This is the edge of the Moon as it begins to pass in front of the Sun. The notch grows larger, and in a few minutes half the Sun is covered. Twilight is now beginning to come over the land.

In a few minutes more, the Moon has covered all but one tiny part of the Sun.

How eclipses happen. During an eclipse of the Sun, the Moon is between the Sun and Earth and covers the Sun. This covering of the Sun by the Moon causes two shadows to form. Each shadow is cone shaped, a small, dark cone within a large, lighter cone. People who are in this darker cone will experience a total eclipse that lasts but a few minutes. People who are in the lighter cone will experience a partial eclipse. During a partial eclipse, the Moon covers only a portion of the Sun.

The end of the world? Some people in ancient times feared that an eclipse meant the end of the world. Some thought a wild beast was eating up the Sun.

This sparkles for an instant and then vanishes. Now, the Earth is dark, and a glorious halo surrounds the black disk of the Moon. This is the Sun's corona. Solar prominences leap out into space, and sunlight shines between mountains at the Moon's edge.

The Moon is traveling fast — 2,000 miles an hour. The eclipse cannot last more than a few minutes. Soon the sparkling diamond appears again, now on the other side of the Moon's disk. The Sun appears as a bright sliver that quickly grows in size. Soon, the Moon passes entirely across the Sun's face, and the Sun is its usual self.

Eclipses take different paths at different times. Sooner or later, just about every person in the world has a chance to see an eclipse. When an eclipse is due in your area, you will probably find reports about it in the newspapers ahead of time.

A total eclipse. This series of pictures shows how an eclipse of the Sun would look at five minute intervals. Notice that the Sun's corona is visible only when the Moon completely hides the Sun's central portion, or photosphere. It is at this time that the part of the Earth in the path of the total eclipse is bathed in a soft, silvery darkness.

7

THE SUN'S FAMILY

THE SUN is the center of a sort of giant merry-go-round. Around and around it travel the nine planets with their moons. Among them is Earth. Also in the merry-go-round are the asteroids, comets, and meteors. All the members of the merry-go-round together are called the Solar System.

Above is a diagram showing the orbits, or curved paths, which the planets follow around the Sun. The diagram shows the order of the planets but not their relative distances from the Sun. To show the relative distances, we would need a page about two miles wide.

If this is hard to believe, let's plan a diagram. Suppose the Sun is a ball 30 inches wide—about as big as the ball on the facing page. Then the planet Mercury is only the size of the letter O, and is about 84 feet away. Some 250 feet away is Earth, as big as a pea. And the planet Pluto, just a little bigger than Mercury, is at a distance of 2 miles.

Following the orbit nearest the Sun is little Mercury, always scorched on the side facing the Sun. Next is cloudy but beautiful Venus; then its twin in size, Earth; and red, mysterious Mars is fourth. The fifth orbit is followed by a stream of asteroids—chunks of rock and metal too small to be called planets. Big Jupiter is the sixth traveler on the merry-go-round. Beyond it are the ringed planets Saturn and Uranus, the green planet Neptune, and finally little Pluto—so far

0   100   1000

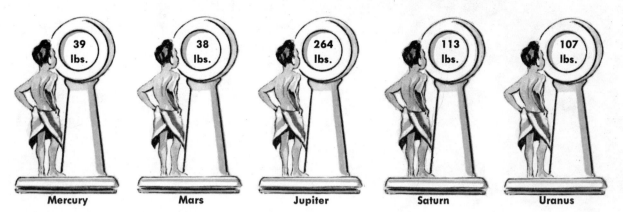

39 lbs.	38 lbs.	264 lbs.	113 lbs.	107 lbs.
Mercury	Mars	Jupiter	Saturn	Uranus

away that it can be seen only through big telescopes.

Between the planets travel other, smaller objects. There are the comets—strange, bright objects whose long tails we sometimes see streaming across the sky. There are clusters of meteors—pieces of metal and stone drifting in space. These sometimes strike the planets as they race along their orbits. And there is also much gas and dust.

The orbit of Mercury, nearest planet to the Sun, is about 72 million miles across. It would take a space rocket four months to cover that distance at a speed of 25,000 miles per hour. The orbit of Pluto is over 7,000 million miles across. Your space rocket would take about 30

years to cover that distance.

Why do the planets keep traveling around the Sun, instead of racing straight off into space? The reason is gravity — the same force that keeps

Distances in the Solar System. If the Sun were the size of this ball, the Earth would be the size of a pea, and 250 feet away.

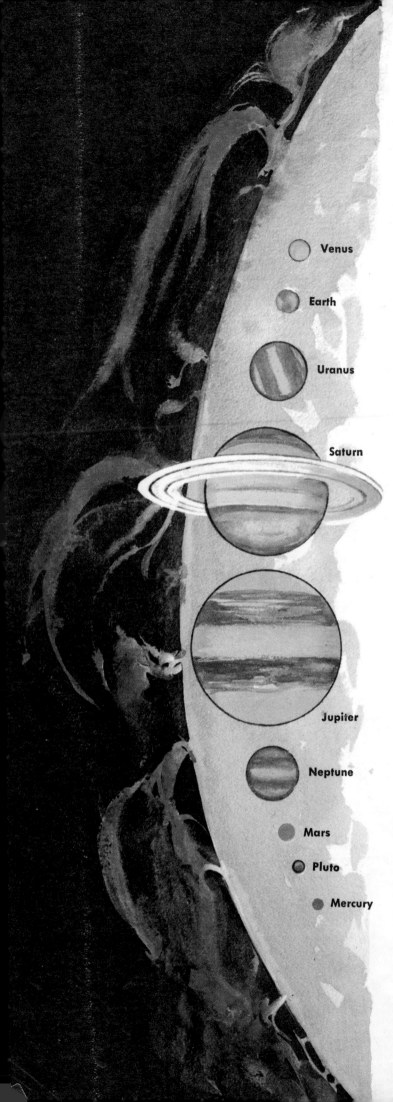

Venus

Earth

Uranus

Saturn

Jupiter

Neptune

Mars

Pluto

Mercury

you on Earth. Everything in the universe, actually, attracts other objects. The Sun is so tremendous that it pulls with enormous force on all the planets. It holds them in their circling paths, just as you can hold onto a pail while swinging it around and around.

But if the Sun is pulling on every planet, and every planet is pulling on every other planet, why don't all the planets get pulled into the Sun?

All moving objects want to move in a straight line in space. If there were no Sun, the Earth and all the other planets would fly off into space, each at their own speed. For Earth, this is 66,600 miles an hour. This wanting to go in a straight line is just balanced by the inward pull of the Sun's gravitational force. As a result, the Earth and all the other planets travel around the Sun.

Long ago, the large members of the Solar System reached this balance among themselves, so that none goes crashing into another. Some asteroids occasionally collide with each other and meteors often hit the Earth, Moon, and most likely some of the other planets. But we can be fairly sure there will be peace and quiet in the Sun's family for a long time.

PLANET FACTS

	Miles in Diameter	Volume Compared to Earth's	Number of Moons	Symbol
Mercury	3,012	1/18	0	☿
Venus	7,530	9/10	0	♀
Earth	7,927		1	⊕
Mars	4,201	1/7	2	♂
Jupiter	85,400	1,249	12	♃
Saturn	71,400	731	10	♄
Uranus	31,200	61	5	♅
Neptune	30,700	58	2	♆
Pluto	3,600?	1/14?	?	♇

MERCURY: THE LITTLEST PLANET

THE SMALLEST planet, only 3,012 miles in diameter, is smaller than two of Jupiter's moons and one of Saturn's moons.

Mercury gets ten times as much sunlight as Earth. As Mercury travels around the Sun, it turns very slowly. On its sunny side, temperatures rise to around 800 degrees — hot enough to melt lead. But there is no atmosphere on the planet to carry heat around to the dark side. This may remain as cold as 260 degrees below zero.

In old legends and myths, the swiftest messenger of the gods was Mercury. The planet is well named, for it is the fastest traveler in the Solar System. It circles the Sun at almost 110,000 miles per hour. In this journey it turns one and one third times, so its day is two thirds as long as its year. While Earth is having 59 days, Mercury is having only one day.

Mercury goes through phases like our Moon's. Sometimes it is a thin crescent, sometimes full and round. But you would need a telescope to see the phases.

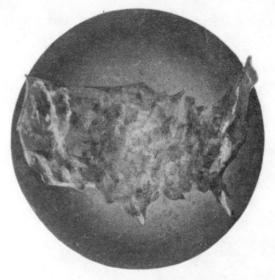

Mercury's size. Mercury is the smallest planet. It is almost large enough to cover the United States.

Even through giant telescopes, astronomers can make out only a few faint lines on Mercury's scorched face. Probably the waterless, airless landscape is quite smooth. The chance for any life at all on this bleak planet is slim.

Being so near the Sun, Mercury is usually hidden by the glare. Six times a year, however, for a few days, it is far enough from the Sun to be seen (if you know just where to look) in the twilight or at dawn as a tiny "star."

On the surface of Mercury. The sunny side of the planet is hot enough to melt lead. The landscape is probably quite smooth. The sky is black because there is no atmosphere to scatter the Sun's rays.

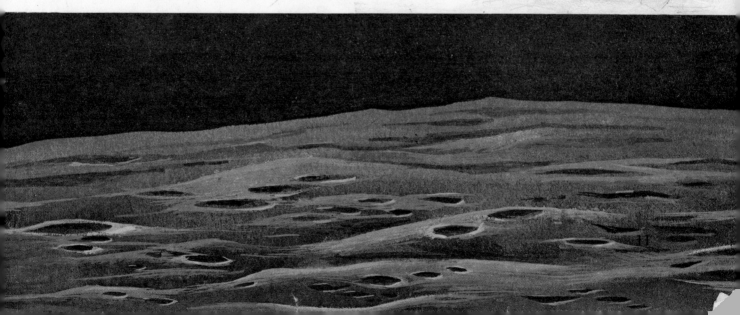

VENUS: THE BRIGHTEST PLANET

VENUS, second planet out from the Sun, is 7,530 miles in diameter — nearly the size of Earth. When between Sun and Earth, Venus is closer to us than any other planet. Yet no one has ever seen its face. This is hidden by thick layers of clouds which never lift. Venus is truly a mystery planet.

While Earth is having 225 days, Venus has its full year, completing its trip around the Sun. Venus turns almost once during this journey. Its day is about as long as its year.

Like Mercury and the Moon, Venus goes through phases. Sometimes it is a "morning star," sometimes an "evening star." When a crescent, it is brighter than any star — so bright that on a very clear, dark night it can cast shadows on the Earth.

When at its brightest, Venus seems to hang like a great white lantern in the evening or early morning sky. It is brighter than any other object in the sky except the Sun and Moon. No wonder the ancients named it Venus, after the goddess of beauty.

In the heavy clouds that cover Venus, astronomers detect carbon dioxide but very little water or oxygen. Beneath the atmosphere, which holds the Sun's heat, the land is much hotter than Earth, because Venus is closer to the Sun—only 67 million miles away.

The American and Russian space probes show that Venus is a very dry place and very hot, with temperatures of about 900 degrees. The air pressure on the surface is about 100 times what it is on Earth: Life as we know it could not exist there.

Venus as "evening star" (upper picture) and "morning star." Venus is an evening star when seen in the west as our part of the Earth turns away from the Sun. It is a morning star when seen in the east as our part of the Earth turns toward the Sun.

EARTH: OUR HOME

THE WORLDS around the Sun are very different from one another. The planets range from giants to pygmies. Some are very hot, some very cold. Some are covered with clouds, others not. The landscapes range from the friendly meadows and hills of Earth to the scorching-hot surface of Mercury and the clouded, stormy ice fields of Jupiter. Earth is probably the only planet where life of the kind we know could exist.

Temperatures in the Solar System range from millions of degrees at the Sun's core to 460 degrees below zero on the outer planets. Even the hottest and coldest temperatures on the Earth are much milder!

Earth is probably the only planet with enough unfrozen water to support animal life. The atmosphere blocks most of the deadly radiation from space, but enough sunlight comes through to make plants grow and to furnish energy for man's machines. The atmosphere protects us against fast-moving meteors. It has the oxygen we need for breathing. And Earth's crust has the many kinds of rocks, minerals, and soils we use for our civilization.

Earth gives us conveniently spaced days and nights. We have seasons. And Earth's gravity is neither too strong nor too weak for us to endure.

Far out among the stars there may be other solar systems—perhaps thousands or millions of them. Even there it might be hard to find a planet friendlier to life than our own good Earth.

A long journey. Earth's orbit around the Sun is nearly a circle, about 560 million miles around. Earth turns, like a top, while going forward at a speed of 18 miles per second. Each complete turn makes one day and one night. Each complete journey around the Sun makes one year.

TIME AND SEASONS

As EARTH moves in its grand, curved path around the Sun, it turns like a top, once in each 24 hours. At every moment during this time exactly half of Earth is in sunlight and half in darkness. Sunlight steadily travels over Earth's face, and almost every spot on the planet has daylight and then darkness.

The time taken by Earth to complete one rotation is called a day. The day has been divided up into 24 parts, or hours. Clocks keep track of the passing of these hours.

The day can be neatly divided up into 24 hours, but the year is a problem. It contains 365 days, with about 6 hours left over. So we add one day to every fourth year to make our calendar fit the Sun's schedule. The year that gets the extra day—February 29—is Leap Year.

Days and nights. The boy in the picture is shining his flashlight on a globe, just as the Sun shines on the Earth. To show how day and night happen, he can slowly turn the globe while he keeps the light on it.

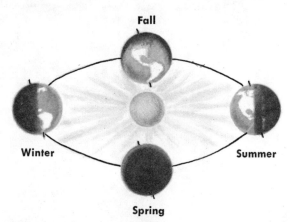

Fall

Winter

Summer

Spring

The seasons. The positions of Earth relative to the Sun give us our seasons. Seasons as named here are for the northern hemisphere. In the southern hemisphere, seasons are opposite.

As Earth makes its yearly journey around the Sun, it keeps a leaning position—like the tilt of globes you have at home or at school. So long as the north pole is leaning toward the Sun, more light falls on the northern hemisphere than on the southern hemisphere. It is summer in the northern hemisphere, winter in the southern. The days are longer in the northern hemisphere, shorter in the southern.

Six months later, Earth is on the opposite side of the Sun. Now the north pole is leaning away from the Sun. Less sunlight reaches the northern hemisphere. We have short winter days.

The shorter days of winter are one reason why winter is colder than summer. Another reason is that in winter, the Sun's path across the sky is nearer the horizon. Its rays strike the Earth more slantingly than in summer. They have to pass through more atmosphere to reach Earth, and more are blocked. Also, the slant makes them spread over a larger area than in summer. The larger the area, the less heat and light any one part of the area gets.

How would it be if Earth had no tilt? There would never be any relief from heat in lands near the equator, and never any relief from cold in lands near the poles. What a world it would be then!

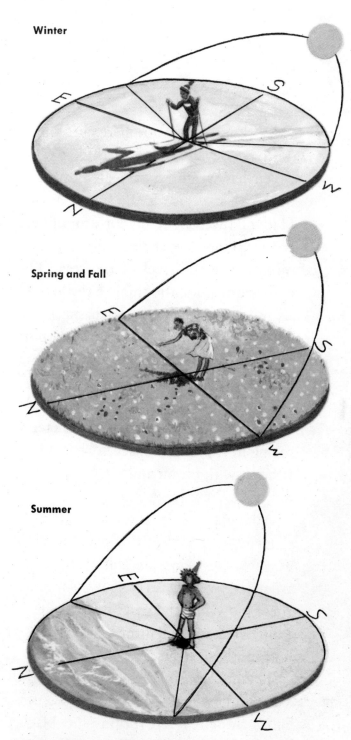

Winter

Spring and Fall

Summer

Why the seasons? In winter, the Sun follows a lower path across the sky than in summer. In spring and fall it follows a path in between.

15

AROUND AND INSIDE EARTH

W E LIVE at the bottom of an ocean of gases that covers the globe. This ocean is the air—our atmosphere. It is made up mostly of the gas nitrogen. A quarter of the atmosphere is oxygen, the part that people and animals need. The rest is carbon dioxide, which plants use, and a few rare gases.

Without the atmosphere, life could not have developed on Earth.

Air has weight. So the air nearest to the earth's surface is the most packed. Half of the weight of our atmosphere is packed into a layer rising three or four miles above the level of the seas. The higher one goes, the thinner the air. At six miles we need an extra air supply to keep alive. For lack of air to support them, balloons and airplanes cannot get higher than about 20 miles.

At 50 miles the air is much thinner. Yet it is here that most of the meteors racing in from outer space are heated by friction with the air and turn into harmless gases. Few reach Earth.

Above 200 miles there is so little air that space is practically empty. But even at 600 miles there are still a few stray particles. When struck by sunlight, these glow like the gases in fluorescent bulbs, forming the auroras, or northern and southern lights.

Beyond 600 miles there is only the very thin gas that is present in the entire Solar System. Here begins the black, cold outer space which man is now crossing on his way to the Moon.

A "slice" of Earth. Man is now exploring the atmosphere with airplanes, rockets, and satellites. In this picture a satellite is seen 1,000 miles above the Earth. Lower is the aurora borealis, or northern lights, caused by sunlight hitting the upper atmosphere. The roots of volcanoes may reach down 100 miles into the Earth. What the Earth is like beneath its crust is still mostly a mystery.

The Earth's crust. Like the wrinkled skin of a dried-up apple, the Earth's crust is only a very thin layer covering the insides.

But what about the inside of Earth? Is it just rock, rock, rock all the way through to China?

The rock crust of Earth is as thin for Earth as an apple skin is thin for the apple. It is made up mostly of the rocks called granite and basalt. The crust cracks into great blocks and layers, which shift up and down over long periods of time. When they shift suddenly, an earthquake occurs.

Earth's diameter is 7,927 miles, but man has tunneled only a short way down into the crust. The deepest mines go down only a few miles. But scientists learn much about the insides of Earth by studying volcanoes and earthquakes. The lava, or melted rock, that flows out of volcanoes comes from deep in Earth and tells us what kinds of rocks are there. Earthquake shocks are recorded on very sensitive instruments called seismographs. These tell the scientist where the Earth's crust has shifted and how strong the shock was.

The deeper one goes into the Earth, the warmer it gets. Much heat comes from radioactive minerals, such as uranium, and from underground pressures. At 5 to 20 miles down, the temperature may be 1,600 degrees. From here, lava works up through cracks and may burst out through the crust as volcanoes. The core of our planet may be nickel and iron in liquid form.

The chance that man can ever get more than a few miles deep into the earth is small. To do his exploring he will have to depend on instruments like the seismograph.

17

OUR NEIGHBOR THE MOON

THE MOON is Earth's closest neighbor in the Solar System. To us it looks about as big as the Sun, but that is only because it is much nearer. A solid ball, it is only 2,160 miles in diameter.

Just as the Sun's gravity keeps the planets circling the Sun, Earth's gravity keeps the Moon going around Earth. Sometimes the Moon is as near to us as 225,727 miles; sometimes it is as far away as 252,002 miles.

The Moon moves at 2,000 miles an hour, but takes nearly a month to make each trip. During that time it rotates only once, and therefore the same side keeps facing Earth. Until 1959, no one had ever seen the other side of the Moon.

The Moon gives out no light of its own. Moonlight is light that has traveled from the Sun to the Moon. The Moon, like a mirror, reflects it.

Because the Moon is nearer Earth than any planet, it was the first object in outer space to be visited by rockets from Earth. Our astronauts found the Moon to be a very unfriendly, though interesting, little world.

Plains of gray rock and dust, high rugged mountains, and craters cover the moon's surface. Long ago, the plains were believed to be seas, but modern telescopes revealed that they were dry. Craters may have been caused by volcanoes and by meteors smashing into

On the Moon. Riding in a lunar rover, our astronauts explored the Moon's surface. As shown here, much of the land is barren, dusty plains dotted with craters. Other areas of the Moon are covered with rugged mountains and large hills.

the Moon from space. Some craters are over 100 miles wide and nearly 5 miles deep. Our astronauts have had trouble getting across this battered land, even using a land rover.

Our astronauts had to carry their own air and water, because the Moon has neither. When moving about, they could jump quite far and lift large rocks. This is because the Moon's gravity is only one-sixth as strong as the Earth's. They have brought back many rocks which scientists hope will help us find out about how the Moon and the Solar System formed.

They had to talk to each other by radio, because the Moon has no atmosphere to carry sounds. They also found no wind, no clouds, no rain—no weather of any kind. The sky is black, even when the Sun is up, because there is no air to scatter the Sun's rays across the sky. If the astronauts did not have protective space suits, the Sun's bright rays would instantly burn any exposed part of the body.

Instruments left on the Moon by the astronauts show that many meteors hit its surface. Had these meteors hurtled into Earth's atmosphere, they would have quickly turned to gas and dust.

In ancient times, the Moon was called Luna, and was believed to be a beautiful goddess. Only a hundred years ago, people thought the Moon must be inhabited, perhaps by beings strange to us. Today, scientists are almost sure that there is no life on the Moon.

The Moon's face. Our eyes alone see only darkish patches on the Moon. With large binoculars we can see features that show in this photograph. Craters and mountains are seen best before the Moon becomes full.

Labels on the moon photograph:
SEA OF COLD, SEA OF SHOWERS, ALPS MTS., POSIDONIUS, APPENINE MTS., SEA OF SERENITY, ARISTARCHUS, COPERNICUS, SEA OF CRISES, KEPLER, SEA OF TRANQUILLITY, OCEAN OF STORMS, SEA OF CLOUDS, PYRENEES MTS., SEA OF HUMORS, ALTAI MTS, TYCHO, LEIBNITZ MTS.

MOON PHASES, ECLIPSES, AND TIDES

As WE watch the Moon from night to night, it seems to change shape. The changing shapes are called phases. They are caused by the constant changing of the Moon's position in the sky in relation to Sun and Earth.

A full half of the Moon is always lighted by the Sun; the other half is always dark. When the Moon moves between Earth and Sun, we cannot see the lighted side. This phase is called New Moon. An evening or so later, as

Phases of the Moon. The diagram shows stages in the Moon's journey around Earth. The photographs show how the Moon looks to us at each stage.

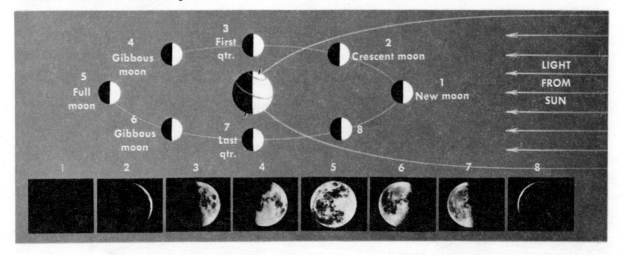

Diagram labels: 4 Gibbous moon, 3 First qtr., 2 Crescent moon, 5 Full moon, 1 New moon, LIGHT FROM SUN, 6 Gibbous moon, 7 Last qtr., 8

the Moon moves on, a thin edge, or crescent, of the lighted side comes into view. Night by night this crescent grows until, when the Moon is a quarter of the way around Earth, we see half of the lighted side. This phase is called First Quarter.

About two weeks after New Moon, the journeying Moon is opposite the Sun and we can see the full lighted side. This is Full Moon. Then, as the Moon moves along the other side of its orbit, we see less and less of the lighted side until the phase of New Moon is reached again.

Sometimes there is an eclipse of the Moon. This happens when the Moon in its journeying passes into the long shadow cast by Earth. The round edge of the shadow slowly moves across the Moon's disk until only half of the disk is still bright, then only a crescent, and finally nothing at all. Then a bright crescent appears on the other edge of the Moon and grows wider. Soon the entire disk is bright again.

The Moon's eclipse lasts an hour or so because the Earth's shadow is much wider than the Moon's disk.

Even when the Moon is completely in Earth's shadow, we can still see its face as a dim reddish disk. This is so

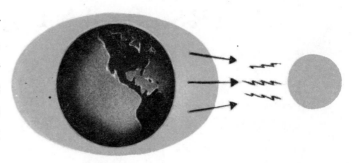

The Moon causes tides. The Moon's gravitational force tugs at the Earth and makes the oceans bulge.

because some sunlight, as it travels through Earth's atmosphere, bends into the Earth's dark shadow and falls upon the Moon.

Just as Earth's gravity pulls at the Moon, so the Moon's gravity pulls at Earth. It is this pull that causes the tides —the rising and falling of the ocean's level. We see this change at the seashore.

The pull of the Moon causes the ocean to bulge toward it. As the Moon travels around Earth, the bulge follows. The bulge is called high tide, and after it passes there is a period of low water called low tide.

The bulge on the side of Earth facing the Moon is matched by another bulge on the opposite side of Earth. Therefore, all seacoasts have two high tides and two low tides each day. It is a little less than six hours from low tide to high, and from high to low.

High tide. When the Moon is halfway between the horizons, the water level is high along the coasts.

Low tide. When the Moon is at the horizon, the water level is low along the coast.

MARS: PLANET OF MYSTERY

BEYOND the orbit of Earth, 141 million miles from the Sun, cruises the red planet, named for the Roman god of war. Men have found it the most fascinating of all the planets, because its face is the easiest to see.

Its diameter of 4,201 miles is a little over half that of Earth. The Martian day is a half hour longer than ours. The year is equal to 687 Earth days.

As Mars and Earth follow their orbits, sometimes Earth comes between Mars and the Sun. Then we are closest to the red planet—as near as 35 million miles. Astronomers all over the world turn their telescopes toward Mars night after night to observe its mysterious face.

The atmosphere of Mars is thin, and clouds are rare. But the planet is small and far away, and the atmosphere of Earth blocks some of its light. Therefore even in big telescopes Mars looks only about as big as a golf ball—and a rather misty one at that. So there has always been a lot of guessing about what the planet's surface is really like.

Because of the Mariner-Mars space probes, we now have many good photographs of the Martian surface. Mars' surface looks much like the Moon's.

Approaching Mars. Straight ahead of our spaceship is the red planet, 13,000 miles away. On our port side, 16 miles off, is the moon Phobos. Small meteors (like the meteor here, at right) have irregular shapes.

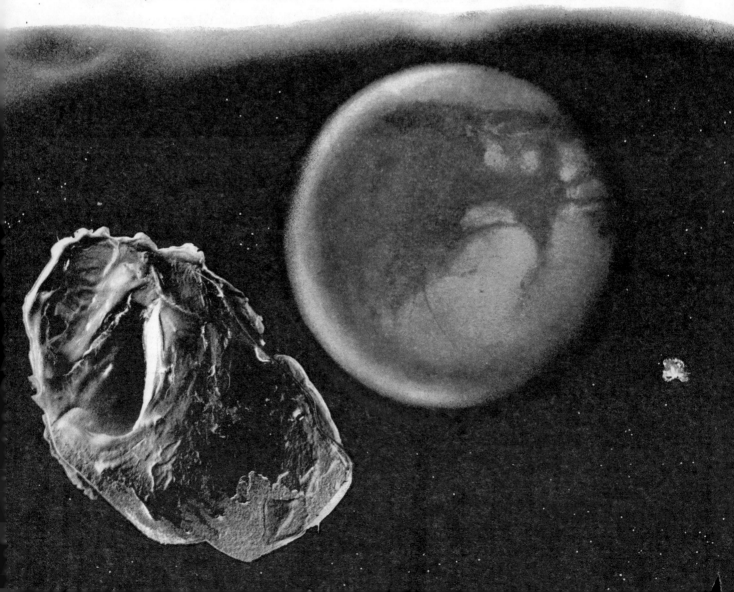

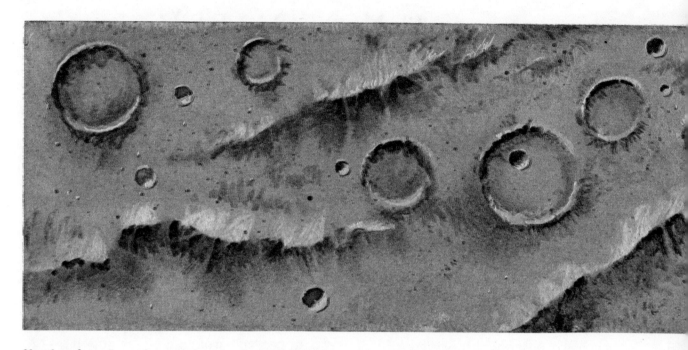

Mars' surface. From photographs taken by various Mariner spacecraft and sent back to Earth, we now know that Mars' surface is much like the Moon's—dry and desolate with many craters dotting the land.

There are some very large volcanoes and very deep canyons on Mars, but most of the surface is dry plain with many craters. Some canyons look like water flowed in them in the past, but now Mars is too dry and cold for any liquid water to be present.

Mars has no rivers, no oceans or lakes. But it has a tilt like Earth's and therefore has seasons. When it is winter in one hemisphere, frozen carbon dioxide and some ice covers the area around the pole. This polar cap is probably less than a foot deep, but it may contain nearly all the water on the planet!

In spring, the ice cap begins to shrink. Through telescopes we see dark, greenish patches appear along the edges of the cap. These are perhaps areas covered by simple plants, but they also could be chemical changes.

As autumn comes, the greenish areas turn brown. As the Martian winter sets in, the polar cap grows again.

Mars' larger moon, Phobos, is only 17 miles in diameter. It rises in the west and sets in the east, and it goes around Mars three times every day at a speed of about 6,000 miles per hour. While our Moon is going around Earth once, Phobos circles Mars 87 times!

Phobos was named for the goddess of fear, a companion of the mythical war god Mars. Its orbit lies only 5,800 miles out from the planet, but even so it would look much smaller in the Martian sky than our Moon looks in the Earth's sky.

The other moon of Mars, about three times as far out, is Deimos. This is the smallest moon in the whole Solar System — only ten miles in diameter. Much slower than Phobos, it circles Mars four times in about five days. Seen from Mars, Deimos at night would look like a dim, distant star.

"MEN OF MARS"

IN 1877 the Italian astronomer Schiaparelli reported seeing regular patterns of lines on the surface of Mars. Since they looked like trenches, he called them "canali," an Italian word which means channels. But he was misunderstood. Soon people were talking about "canals" and the "men of Mars."

Even astronomers were excited. In the United States a famous astronomer named Percival Lowell raised the money to build an observatory at Flagstaff, Arizona, to observe the planets and, incidentally, to settle the argument about Mars. The observatory, named for

Martian seasons. Like Earth, Mars keeps a tilted position as it journeys around the Sun. Therefore it has seasons. Here we see one polar cap shrinking and the other one growing as the seasons pass.

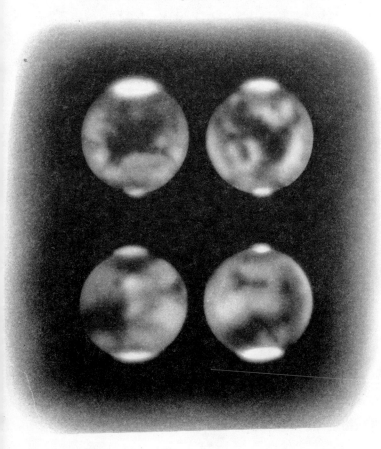

Lowell, was completed in 1894. It has done great work for astronomy, but the arguments about Mars are still not completely settled.

In 1956, Mars came closer to Earth than it had come in many years. Astronomers all over the world watched it through telescopes, photographed it, and studied its light with spectroscopes. Still they found no sure sign that there is any life on Mars. The "canals" are not so regular as they seemed. They appeared broken and as much as 30 miles wide—too wide for real canals.

Today, astronomers believe there are no people on Mars. The Mariner-Mars space probes reveal a dry planet with volcanoes, canyons, and many craters. Mars has very little water and certainly no canals or other signs of civilization.

People like ourselves could not live on the red planet. Its atmosphere has no oxygen worth mentioning. The atmosphere is very thin—it could barely support simple plants.

The probability that plants live on Mars was once an argument for the "canals." People said the "canals" must be irrigation ditches to lead water from the melting snow caps to farmers' fields. But few astronomers today take these ideas seriously.

In the near future, unmanned spacecraft will land on Mars' surface. They will contain instruments that will test the land to see if simple plants or animals live there. But it is doubtful that even these can exist on Mars' barren surface.

But even if there are no people on Mars, we can look forward to the day when Earthmen may explore it.

They will find desert land, waterless except around the polar cap. They will have to carry their own oxygen for breathing. Sometimes they will have to battle great dust storms.

The clear daytime sky will not look like Earth's sky. The thin atmosphere will have a deep blue or violet color. The Sun will look smaller than it does from our Earth, and will give less heat and light.

The very thin atmosphere of Mars means that temperatures fall very low at night—perhaps to 100 degrees below zero. Also because of the thinness of the air the stars would seem very bright, and would twinkle less.

Although the planet is much warmer in daylight, it never gets really hot. In spring at noon, the temperature at the equator may warm up to 50 degrees. The hottest day in summer probably would be 80 degrees or so.

Mars is not an inviting planet, but it seems friendlier than the others, and it remains the one that men want most to visit. Mars is closer to us than all other planets, except Venus. And, of course, it seems possible to get there. Man has already visited the Moon. Mars will surely be the next port of call.

Three drawings of Mars (at right). In the past, observers could sometimes see details on the planet more clearly than the details could be photographed. Many of the best early views of Mars were drawings. Today, photographs taken by the Mariner-Mars space probes show Mars' surface in greater detail than has ever been seen.

Mars as drawn by Christian Huyghens, August 13, 1672.

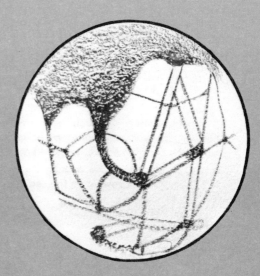

The "canals" as drawn by Schiaparelli, June 4, 1888.

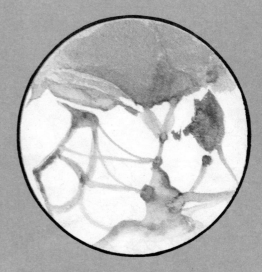

An observer's view of Mars, drawn in 1954.

25

JUPITER: KING OF PLANETS

MIGHTY Jupiter, largest world in the Sun's family, was named after the Roman god. Ten Earths lined up in a row would not be quite enough to cross the face of Jupiter. The big planet, weighing over 300 times as much as Earth, is 85,400 miles in diameter at its equator. If hollow, Jupiter could hold all the planets except Saturn.

When closest to Earth, Jupiter is still over 400 million miles away. Almost 500 million miles separate it from the Sun. Little sunlight, therefore, reaches the big planet. The atmosphere, thousands of miles deep and full of thick clouds of poisonous gases, hides Jupiter's surface. No plant or animal from Earth could live in that atmosphere. If they didn't die from ammonia and methane gases, they would soon freeze.

As seen in a telescope, Jupiter's clouds are banded or streaked with pale red, yellow, and brown. An odd feature is the Great Red Spot, some 25,000 miles wide, which was noticed over 100 years ago and is now fading. Scientists think that the spot is a "hot air" storm.

Jupiter's rotation speed is so fast that the planet bulges a good deal at its equator. Astronomers learned the speed by

Visitors to Jupiter. Although space travelers might not be able to land on the planet, they could land on one of its larger moons. These moons may be somewhat like our own Moon. The little picture at upper left compares the sizes of the Earth and the Great Red Spot.

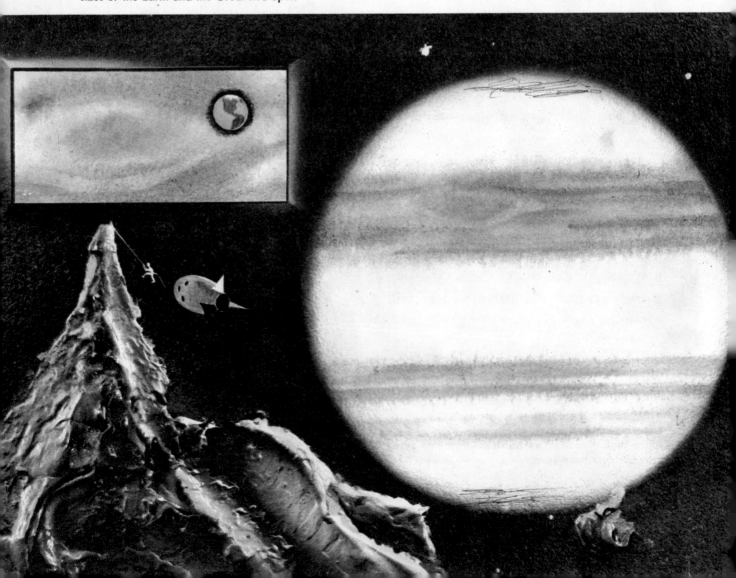

timing the Red Spot. One rotation is completed in about 10 hours. The day is short, but the year is 12 times as long as Earth's.

Astronomers are not sure what Jupiter's surface is like. But the planet's size, the pull of its gravity on its moons and other planets, and its motions give them clues. Probably Jupiter has a core of liquid hydrogen, surrounded by frozen hydrogen thousands of miles deep, and then a "slush" of liquid and frozen hydrogen.

It's hard to imagine how any spaceship could land on Jupiter. As the giant planet's powerful gravity pulled the ship downward, it would grow darker and darker outside because of the increasing thickness of the clouds. Finally the ship would probably be crushed by the enormous pressure of Jupiter's atmosphere. Even if the spaceship could survive the great pressure of the atmosphere, it would sink in the hydrogen "slush."

The great Italian thinker Galileo, first to study the sky with a telescope, discovered four moons of Jupiter in 1610. Since then eight more have been discovered. Jupiter has more moons than any other planet. Some are only a few miles in diameter, but two—Ganymede and Callisto—are larger than the planet Mercury. Some moons may be made of rock, others entirely of ice. The twelve follow a very complicated maze of orbits around the planet.

When seen in the night sky, Jupiter looks like a large white star. It is brighter than any other planet except Venus.

Watching the four large moons through telescopes is a favorite activity of amateur astronomers. Sometimes all the moons are at one side of the planet. Then they are seen to move, one by one, behind or in front of the great disk. When a moon moves in front, its shadow is seen creeping across the clouds.

Jupiter in photographs. These two pairs of photographs were taken about 3 weeks apart. Notice the changes in the appearance of the banded clouds.

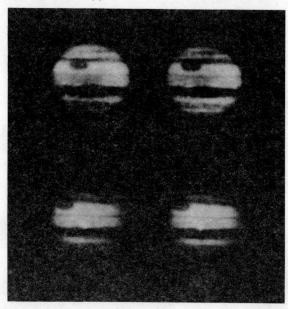

ASTEROIDS: TINY "PLANETS"

IN THE fifth circle around the Sun we find not one planet but a whole stream of very small ones. These are called asteroids, or planetoids. The largest, Ceres, is only 480 miles in diameter. Few are 100 miles through. Many are no larger than a hill or a mountain. Racing around their orbits at many miles per second, the asteroids form a sort of giant necklace around the Sun.

Asteroids are so small that they have little gravity and no atmosphere. Their gravity has not been strong enough to pull these bodies into a neat ball shape.

Too small to be seen well even in big telescopes, asteroids are believed to be ragged and irregular. Probably they consist mostly of rock, iron, and nickel.

At least 1,600 asteroids have been named or given numbers. More are discovered each year—as streaks on photographs taken of the sky. There are so many unimportant small ones that astronomers don't bother to trace them.

A few asteroids have orbits that sometimes bring them within a few million miles of Earth—nearer than any other celestial object except the Moon.

A medium-sized asteroid. There are probably thousands of asteroids as large as the one illustrated here and several hundred that are much larger. However, the number that are the size of a boulder or smaller may be in the billions.

Meteors little and big. Meteors come in all sizes. Most of them burn and break up as they streak through the sky and never reach the ground in one piece.

METEORS: VISITORS FROM SPACE

HAVE YOU ever seen a shooting star? It falls across the dark sky, leaving a silvery trail of light behind. This lasts only for an instant, and is gone.

"Shooting stars" are not really stars. They are meteors. Meteors are the junk of the Solar System. They are scattered among the planets like gravel. Most are no bigger than peas. Some are made of stone; others are nickel or iron. Millions and millions of them shoot into Earth's atmosphere every day. But only a few ever reach the ground.

Meteors shoot into our atmosphere at speeds as great as 45 miles per second. They travel so fast that even in the very thin upper atmosphere there is great friction. Friction, which is the rubbing of objects against each other, produces heat. Most meteors get so hot that they turn into gas or break up into dust as

they fall. In this way our atmosphere protects us against showers of rock and metal that could be very dangerous.

Astronomers estimate that at least 1,000 tons of meteors enter Earth's atmosphere each day. A very few meteors are so big that even if they break up, some pieces reach the ground. These pieces are called meteorites.

Meteors may be odds and ends left over from the creation of the Solar System. Or the remains of a destroyed planet or comets. Or they may be all of these things.

You can see meteors almost any night of the year. About ten per hour are visible. The best time to look is after midnight. Many meteors occur in swarms, or "showers." There are large showers of meteors in August, October, November, and December.

Approaching the ringed planet. Space travelers may someday see Saturn like this—at a distance of about 250,000 miles. At the upper left Earth is compared for size with reddish Titan, Saturn's largest moon.

SATURN: THE RINGED PLANET

THE SIXTH planet out from the Sun is the most beautiful in the Sun's family. The bright yellow cloud-covered globe, with the shimmering rings around it, is magnificent to see. Unfortunately, a telescope is needed to see them. Only one other planet, Uranus, has rings.

The globe is 71,400 miles in diameter. The distance across the rings is over 120,000 miles, but they are quite thin—so thin that the light of stars can come through them. Probably they are about 10 miles thick. There are four main rings—two bright outer ones and two dark inner ones. It is the sunlight striking the rings that makes them shine. They reflect sunlight just as the planets do.

The rings are known to consist of billions upon billions of small particles perhaps the size of gravel, traveling around the planet like a swarm of moons. The nearer they are to the planet, the faster they are moving. They reflect light in a way that indicates they may contain small pieces of ice. Perhaps they are the remains of a tiny former moon that broke up, or are material left over from the time when the planet formed.

Sometimes Saturn is turned so that we see the rings edgewise. Then they almost disappear. Only a thin line of light shows where they are.

Of Saturn's ten moons, Titan is the largest. It is the biggest moon in the Solar System and the only one that is known to have an atmosphere. However, this atmosphere like Jupiter's is full of the poison gases methane and ammonia.

Saturn's tenth moon, Janus, orbits

right on the outer edge of the rings. It was first discovered in 1905, then "lost," then found again in 1966.

The Sun is very far from Saturn—over 885 million miles away. Beneath Saturn's banded clouds the temperature is probably 200 or 300 degrees below zero, and the planet is probably covered with frozen hydrogen thousands of miles thick. Beneath the ice Saturn may have a core like Jupiter's, but smaller.

Saturn is the second largest of all the planets. Only Jupiter has a greater volume. But because so much of the ringed planet is hydrogen, its gravity is much weaker than one would expect. If you weigh 100 pounds on little Earth, you would weigh only 17 pounds more on giant Saturn. On Jupiter you would weigh a total of 264 pounds.

Like Jupiter, Saturn spins fast. Its day is only 10½ hours long. A year on this planet equals 29½ Earth years. It takes that long for Saturn to complete its long journey around the Sun.

Like Jupiter, Saturn would be a hard planet to explore. The pressure of the atmosphere would crush any spaceships we can now build. Future space travelers may have to be satisfied with simply cruising around the great planet. Or, they might find it possible to establish a base on Titan. This moon is 758,000 miles from the planet.

Saturn is the most distant planet that can be easily seen without a telescope. Men have known Saturn for hundreds of years. The Romans gave the planet its name, calling it Saturn after their god of the harvests.

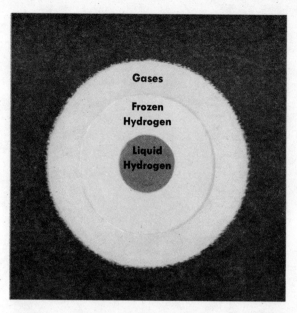

Inside Saturn. This planet is a giant compared to Earth, but weighs little more than Earth. Saturn is believed to consist mostly of the light element hydrogen.

Saturn from different angles. Like Earth, Saturn keeps a tilted position as it travels around the Sun. So the angle from which we see Saturn keeps changing.

The world's greatest telescope—in 1786. This giant reflector was constructed by Sir William Herschel.

THE OUTER PLANETS

URANUS, 1,781 million miles from the Sun, is so far off that even on a dark, clear night it looks like a very faint star.

This planet was discovered accidentally by the English astronomer William Herschel in 1781. Herschel noticed a "star" that was gradually changing its position from month to month, while the other stars kept their regular positions. Herschel knew that true stars do move, but are so far away that their positions seem to remain the same, year after year. So he knew the moving object was not a star. It was a planet.

Uranus, 31,200 miles in diameter, is so far from the Sun that it receives only 1/350th as much sunlight as Earth does. Beneath its thick, green clouds it must be very cold.

A day on Uranus is 10 hours and 45 minutes long. This planet's year equals 84 Earth years.

You will remember the tilt of Earth, which causes our seasons. Uranus has such a great tilt that you might say it rolls on its side. In 1977, astronomers discovered that Uranus has rings similar to Saturn's rings.

Five moons accompany Uranus. Even the largest, Titania, is much smaller than our Moon. As Uranus journeys through space on its side, these moons circle the planet like the seats of a Ferris wheel.

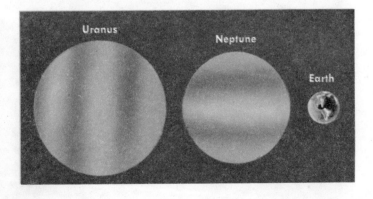

The two outermost planets, Neptune and Pluto, were found only after long searching—and because scientists decided they *must* exist!

After the discovery of Uranus, astronomers studied its motions. They suspected it was being pulled by the gravity of some planet farther out.

The search for another planet began. Finally, in the year 1846 the British astronomer J. C. Adams and the French astronomer U. J. J. Leverrier, working separately, figured out where the unknown planet must be. A telescope at the Berlin Observatory in Germany was turned toward the suspected part of the sky. There was Neptune!

Shrouded like Uranus in greenish clouds, Neptune is so far from the Sun —2,794 million miles—that it is practically as cold as the absolute cold of outer space. The diameter is 30,700 miles. Two moons ride through the black sky with Neptune, one larger than our Moon. A day on Neptune is about 15 hours; a year equals 165 Earth years.

After the discovery of Neptune, astronomers found the motions of Uranus still puzzling. Furthermore, the motions of Neptune, too, were unexpected. Was there still another planet farther out?

At last, in 1930, the discovery was

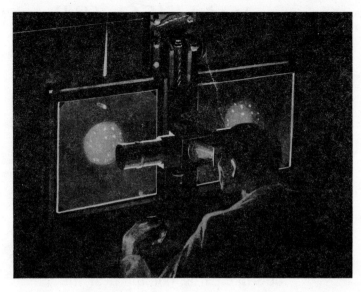

The blink microscope. Astronomers use this instrument to compare photographs of the sky.

made. Clyde Tombaugh, a young astronomer at Lowell Observatory, had been studying the suspected part of the sky. He compared photographs of that part of the sky taken at different times. He noticed one "star" that had moved. It was no star—it was the unknown planet!

The new planet, named Pluto, is about 3,700 million miles from the Sun. Its diameter is estimated to be 3,600 miles. From Pluto the Sun would be seen only as a bright star. The day on Pluto is believed to equal six Earth days; the year, 248 Earth years.

Even Pluto does not entirely explain Neptune's motions. Possibly there is another planet even farther out.

Lowell Observatory Photograph

Mystery solved! These are the two photographs on which Pluto was discovered. The arrows show how it had moved against the unchanging background of stars.

COMETS: TRAMPS OF THE SKY

About two or three times in your life you may have the chance to see a comet. These beautiful travelers blaze through the sky like super skyrockets, leaving behind a trail of light that may be millions of miles long.

Comets are sometimes called tramps of the Solar System because they do not follow nearly circular paths around the Sun as planets do. They follow long, loop-like paths, coming near the Sun at one end and going far out toward the edge of the Solar System at the other end.

The main part of a comet is the head. This is a ball of stony material, dust, and gas loosely held together by gravity. It is much smaller than a planet.

When a comet comes near the Sun, it grows a tail. This is a train of thin gases coming out from the head. Particles of sunlight strike the head, force

some gases out of it, and make them glow as a neon sign does.

Some comets have two tails; a few have more. One comet had nine!

The tail of a comet always points away from the Sun. The pressure of sunlight is the probable reason. As the comet goes farther away from the Sun, pressure lessens, and the tail disappears.

There are thousands of comets, but only a few are big enough or come near enough to Earth to be seen without a telescope.

When first seen, a comet is a faint hazy spot in the dark sky. Night by night it grows brighter, and its position changes. After weeks or months it is at its brightest. Then it gradually fades away.

Some comets return again and again. Many are seen once and no more. Some continue their journeys in space without nearing Earth again. A few comets do break apart, and some of these fall to Earth as a meteor shower.

Most famous is Halley's Comet. Its orbit was figured out by the English astronomer Edmund Halley in 1682. About every 77 years this comet returns to our part of the Solar System. It was last seen in 1910.

A comet's tail is thinner than air. The stars can easily be seen through it. Once when the tail of Halley's Comet swept over Earth, no one except the astronomers even noticed it. If the comet head had hit us, there would have been a different story!

A long time ago people thought comets meant bad luck. So they kept records of comet visits. Such records tell us that Halley's Comet was seen almost 2,000 years ago. Perhaps you will have a chance to see it in 1986.

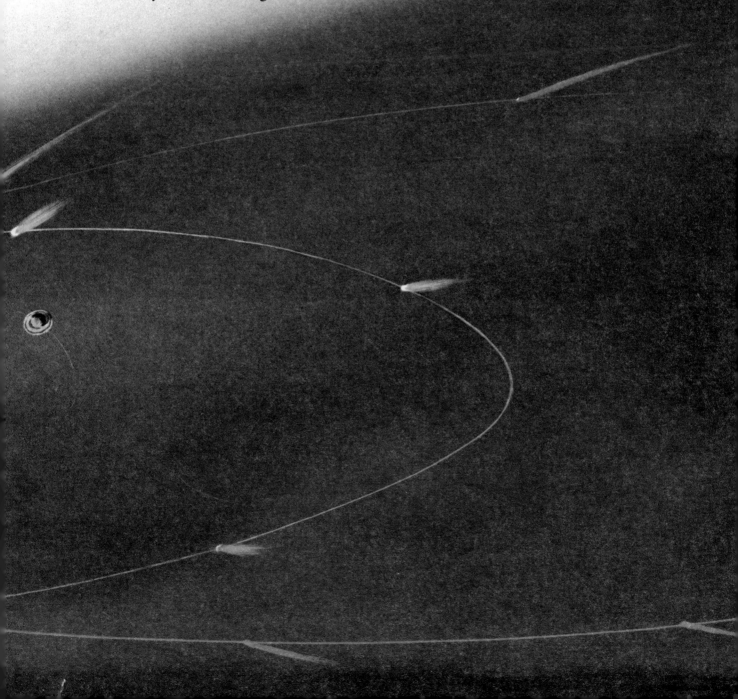

1. Swirling cloud of gas and dust drifts through space.

4. Sun uses up hydrogen, swells, and swallows up nearby planets.

5. Sun shrinks and becomes white dwarf in lifeless Solar System.

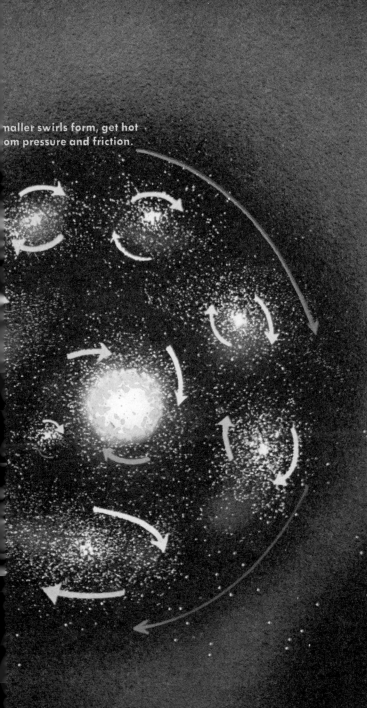

maller swirls form, get hot
om pressure and friction.

BIRTH AND DEATH OF THE SOLAR SYSTEM

THE SOLAR SYSTEM perhaps began five billion years ago as a giant cloud of gas and dust in space. Slowly, gravity drew gas and dust particles together. Swirls formed and got hot from pressure and friction. The biggest became the Sun. Others became planets and smaller members of the Solar System.

Perhaps ten billion years from now the Sun will have little hydrogen left. It may swell enormously, swallowing up the inner planets. Then it may shrink and become a white dwarf star, with lifeless planets circling it for billions of years more.

3. Hottest swirl (center) becomes Sun. Others are planets.

One of the world's largest telescopes. The great Hale reflecting telescope on Palomar Mountain, in southern California, magnifies over 1,000 times. It gathers 360,000 times as much light as the human eye.

TELESCOPES

THE FIRST telescope was made in Holland about 1600. The first person to use such an instrument to study the sky was the great Italian thinker Galileo, in 1609. He was delighted to see craters and mountains of the Moon, the rings of Saturn, and Jupiter with its four larger satellites. Ever since, the telescope has been the main tool of astronomers.

The giant telescopes of our time are very complicated, but the basic idea is simple. Each telescope has an "objective"—a slightly hollowed mirror or a disk of clear, curved glass. Upon this falls light from the object being looked at. This light is then reflected by the mirror (or is bent as it passes through the clear glass) so that the rays come together like a V. At the point of the V is a magnifying lens, or eyepiece.

The larger the objective, the greater is the amount of light from the sky object that falls on it. The greater the amount of light received, the more and the better the object can be magnified. The Hale telescope on Palomar Mountain, in California, has a 200-inch-wide mirror which can collect 360,000 times as much light as the human eye can. It will make an object such as a planet look more than 1,000 times wider than when the eye alone sees it. Stars are so far away that they are still points of light even when magnified 1,000 times.

Telescopes that have a mirror for the objective are called reflectors. Those

38

which use a clear lens are refractors. Big telescopes have a clock mechanism to keep the telescope aimed at the right part of the sky while Earth rotates.

The 200-inch Hale telescope and a 240-inch Russian telescope are the two largest in the world. Both are reflecting telescopes. The Hale can detect stars so far away that their light has taken two billion years to reach us!

Our atmosphere scatters much of the light that comes from stars and planets. A telescope magnifies this scattering. For this reason, telescopes larger than these two may never be built.

Large telescopes are mostly in university observatories. These are usually located on a high hill, far from city lights. On every clear night the big "scopes" are kept working constantly. Planets, stars, comets, and other objects are watched, photographed, and mapped. During daylight hours, observatory workers are busy with information which the telescope has given them.

Observatories have been built in most large countries. They constantly exchange useful information. Hundreds of amateur astronomers, too, study the sky with their small telescopes and make reports to the observatories.

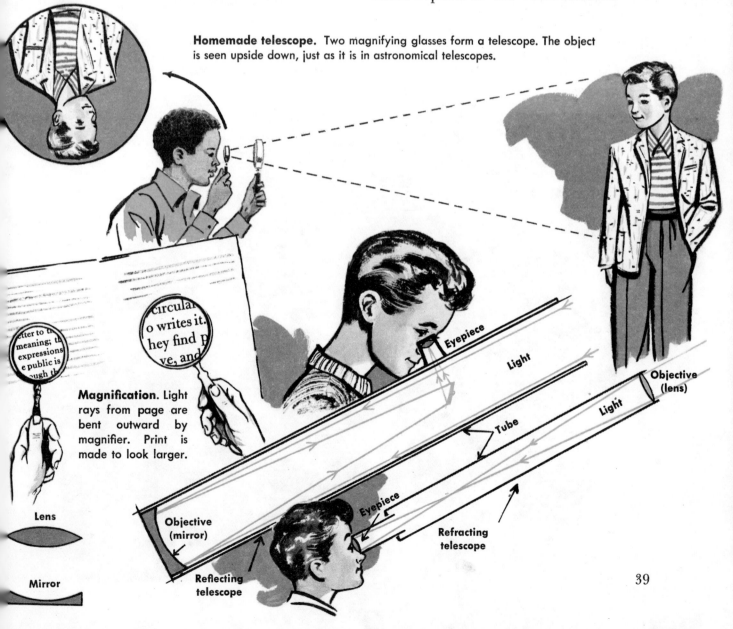

Homemade telescope. Two magnifying glasses form a telescope. The object is seen upside down, just as it is in astronomical telescopes.

Magnification. Light rays from page are bent outward by magnifier. Print is made to look larger.

Lens

Mirror

Eyepiece

Light

Objective (lens)

Tube

Light

Objective (mirror)

Eyepiece

Refracting telescope

Reflecting telescope

THE ZODIAC

Anyone can learn to recognize in the sky not only Sun and Moon, but also other members of the Sun's family— planets, meteors, and sometimes even asteroids and comets. But first one must understand how these objects move.

The Earth is a great ball surrounded by millions of stars at very great distances. From an open field at night we see about half of the sky, like a giant umbrella overhead. Because the Earth is rotating, the stars cross the sky as the hours pass.

The stars seem to form patterns, which are called constellations. These stay almost exactly the same, year after year. The stars are so far away that they have to move billions and billions of miles before we can notice it.

This is the clue to locating the planets. For the planets are much nearer to us than the stars are, and we can notice their movements in front of the constellations from week to week.

Circling the sky from east to west is a sort of pathway of constellations which the Sun, Moon, and planets always follow. The constellations of this pathway, known as the Zodiac, are pictured on the opposite page.

The sky at night. The heavens arch over us like a giant umbrella, with the stars all around the inside, and the North Star at the point. The boy in the picture is facing north. When he turns the umbrella counterclockwise (right to left), he shows how the real stars in the sky seem to move in circles around the North Star.

OUR GALAXY

OUR SUN is just one member of an enormous flattened cluster of stars which astronomers call the Galaxy. This cluster of suns is drifting through space with a slow pinwheeling motion.

The Galaxy has about 100 billion stars in it. If you could see them all and count 3 per second, it would take you over 1,000 years to finish the counting.

Stars are of many colors—blue, white, orange, yellow, red. Many are about the size of our Sun, though some are a thousand times bigger. All are hot balls of churning gases.

All the stars you can see on a dark night are in the Galaxy. During a whole night you would see about 5,000 parade across the heavens. The rest are too far away to see, or are veiled by dust in space, or are hidden by the Earth.

As you know, light travels 186,000 miles per second. That's fast enough to travel around the Earth eight times in one second. But the nearest star to our Sun is much farther away than that. It is so far away that light takes over four years to cover the distance.

Are most stars that far apart? They are. They are scattered so widely that light takes 100,000 years to travel from one side of the Galaxy to the other.

In such a tremendous universe, our Sun doesn't seem very important. From a space ship cruising along the edges of the Galaxy, you probably could not see our Sun even if you knew just where to look. (The cross in the picture shows where.) Our Sun would be just one star among 100 billion. And even if you could spot our "home star," you certainly couldn't see any planets. They are tiny compared to most stars, and shine weakly.

The Galaxy is unbelievably enormous. Yet it is just one star cloud among many. There are millions and millions of other galaxies, reaching as far out into space as the largest telescope can "see." The farthest galaxies are so distant that their light takes two billion years to reach us. Astronomers estimate there are more stars in all the galaxies than there are grains of sand on Earth.

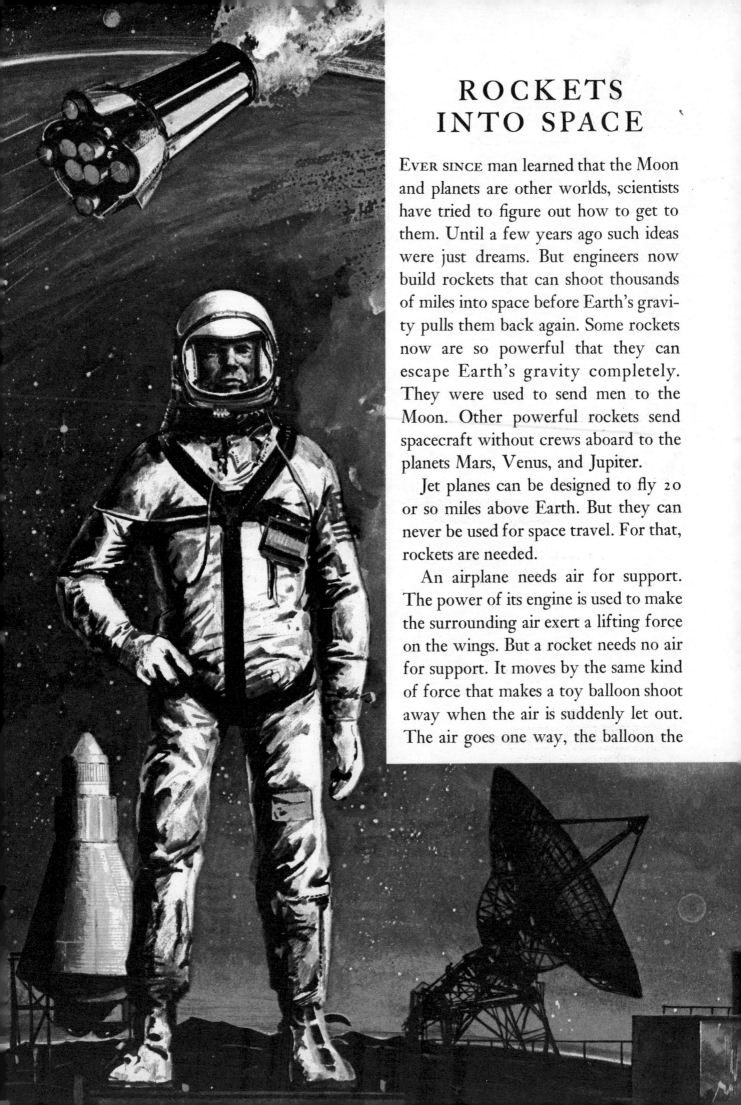

ROCKETS INTO SPACE

EVER SINCE man learned that the Moon and planets are other worlds, scientists have tried to figure out how to get to them. Until a few years ago such ideas were just dreams. But engineers now build rockets that can shoot thousands of miles into space before Earth's gravity pulls them back again. Some rockets now are so powerful that they can escape Earth's gravity completely. They were used to send men to the Moon. Other powerful rockets send spacecraft without crews aboard to the planets Mars, Venus, and Jupiter.

Jet planes can be designed to fly 20 or so miles above Earth. But they can never be used for space travel. For that, rockets are needed.

An airplane needs air for support. The power of its engine is used to make the surrounding air exert a lifting force on the wings. But a rocket needs no air for support. It moves by the same kind of force that makes a toy balloon shoot away when the air is suddenly let out. The air goes one way, the balloon the other. In a rocket, the burning fuel produces gases that blast out from one end and force the rocket ahead.

A rocket can keep going right up through the atmosphere and beyond — until its fuel runs out. If it gets far enough out into space, the force of its outward motion just balances the Earth's pull. Such a rocket could coast around Earth for a long time.

No single stage rocket yet built is powerful enough to completely escape Earth's gravity. However, two or more rockets can be built into one unit. The first rocket carries the unit far up in the atmosphere. When its fuel is gone, this rocket drops away, and the second stage fires. This gives the unit another long, strong push, and when this rocket burns out a third one may take over. In this way it is possible to send a spaceship out far enough so that Earth cannot pull it back.

All of our space missions use rockets with two or more stages. The most powerful rockets built so far were those used to send the astronauts to the Moon. A similar rocket was used to launch Skylab, our first space station.

45

TO OTHER WORLDS

WHY SHOULD men want to visit any of our neighbor planets? The trip would be dangerous and long, lasting months or years. And once the space travelers got to their destination, what then? Even Mars and Venus, judging from what we know of them, don't seem inviting for human visitors. And, on any other planet, unprotected travelers would be quickly frozen, roasted, or smothered by poisonous gases.

But man is determined to master space. New and powerful rockets are being developed. We have already reached the Moon. Important information has been obtained from our Moon trips. Unmanned spaceships have reached the planets Venus, Mars, and Jupiter. Future unmanned spacecraft will travel to the more distant planets.

Astronomers are less optimistic about man traveling in space than are storytellers. Engineers have built a rocket that can escape from the Earth, can travel to the Moon, and can bring its

Distances in the universe. Man may visit the Moon and possibly even one of the nearer planets during your lifetime. But distances beyond the Solar System may never be conquered.

To Pluto.
3,600 million miles

To Mars
35 million miles

To Moon
240,000 miles

To Nearest Star
26 million million miles

crew back. Traveling to the planets and beyond will bring many new problems.

The greatest problem is distance—and time. For example, consider a trip to Mars. A spaceship could not travel there in a straight line, but even if it could, a trip at 25,000 miles an hour would take two months. A journey to Pluto at a million miles an hour would take five months.

Many stories tell about journeys to the stars. If man ever develops space-ships that can go as fast as the speed of light, 186,000 miles per second, it will still take over four years to get to Prox-ima Centauri, the nearest star. Such a trip would be interesting, because this star (really it is two stars very close to-gether) is believed to have at least one large planet circling it. But nine years for a round trip is a long time!

Other stories tell of voyages to neigh-bor galaxies—to universes like our own Milky Way home. The nearest ones are about 150,000 light years away. The light we see left them when mankind was still living in caves.

If we cannot get to the stars, how about reaching them by radio? Scien-tists have succeeded in bouncing radar waves off the Moon, Mars, Venus, and Mercury. Some astronomers think there must be millions upon millions of planets among the billions of stars in our galaxy. If there are living beings on any of these planets, perhaps some of them could re-ceive radio messages from us and make replies. What are the chances?

Radio messages take as long to travel through space as light does. If we could send out a message powerful enough to reach a planet of Proxima Centauri, it would take over four years to arrive. And we don't know whether anyone would be there to get our message or to return it.

Few stars are as near our Earth as five or ten light years. Their planets—if they have any—may have no living things able to answer us. The best guess is that during the twentieth century, at least, man will not succeed in talking to other worlds.

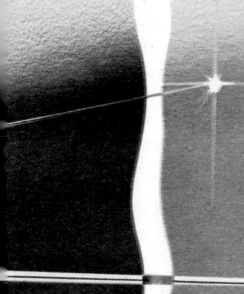

**To Nearest Galaxy
480,000 million million miles**

Skylab

MAN-MADE MOONS

ROCKETS can be used to shoot artificial satellites up into the sky. A satellite is any object that revolves around another object, being held in its orbit by the force of gravity. It is a moon. An artificial satellite is a man-made one.

For years scientists worked on plans for shooting satellites into orbits around Earth. Finally, in 1957, the Russians put their first Sputnik into orbit. Early in 1958 the United States succeeded with its first Explorer.

Since then, man has placed many satellites in orbit around the Earth. He also has placed satellites in orbit around the Moon, Venus, and Mars. But his most important satellite is Skylab.

Skylab is our first space station and the largest satellite to ever circle around our Earth. Skylab is as big as a five-room house and weighs 28 tons. At different times and for varying lengths of time, a three-man crew has lived in Skylab.

They conducted many experiments and have taken thousands of pictures of the Earth and the Sun. Information obtained from Skylab will help scientists learn more about our Earth and the Sun. Scientists are also learning how long man can live in space. This information is important to know if man is to explore space beyond the Moon.

The Skylab space station is only the beginning. In the future, bigger and better space stations will orbit our Earth. Rockets will be put together and launched from these space stations. Since a rocket will not have to overcome as much gravity, the take-off will be easier. Because there is no atmosphere in space, the rocket will be able to work up great speed without using much fuel. Trips to the Moon and beyond might then become common.

The age of space travel and exploration is here!